A MIND'S FACE

A Collection of Original Poems

By Stephen G. Colvin

PublishAmerica
Baltimore

ISBN: 1-4241-5419-7
PUBLISHED BY PUBLISHAMERICA, LLLP
www.publishamerica.com
Baltimore

Printed in the United States of America

For Deb,
my muse.

A MIND'S PACE

MUS(E)SINGS

She seeds
my heart
and voicing
spring
gives birth to
silver green
and twisted
reach of vine
meandering through
my arteries
in a vein passage
to my mind.

Mine eye
is a filtered
lens
that sees
in ways
alien to some
but true
to her
wayfaring ways.

She has shown me
how dreams look
in harsh light
of day
or how they breed
in solitude
to torture
the dispossessed.

She has given
soul,
to my thin
wanton voice
and made it thick
like oak
and fruitful
as an acorn.

She has pushed me
beyond the space
of me
to move with
elders
circles, circles, circles
and deserts
rich with life.

She has spoken to me
in languages
of metaphor,
often cryptic
and undead dreams
of youth
arisen pale.

She has pulled me
from brink to brink
to the arrogant edges
where insight
kisses the ass
of reason
just to offer me
some small
reward.

She writes in me
what will not
speak
but longs to
breathe
like clouds
must breathe
in the cold thin air
where pretensions
suffocate.

She woos me
ever
with promises
of verse
but in truth
I am but her
door man
watching all her
eagles fly.

HOPE MOVES

Hope moves
without grace
without rhythm
without wheels.
It stumbles and staggers
like a drunken man
grasping at the steady hand
of charity.
All color pales
beneath the glaring eye
of scrutiny;
and judgment
the hammer
forges link
upon link.
Against the anvil of conformity
all metal runs
down
the painted whore
walks on staggered heels
hands flailing aimlessly.

HIP

I could wear you
like fashion,
something trendy
and eye catching
a way to impress
the kids.
Like grocery store sushi
you're the new John Belushi
just dieing
to get a laugh.
You're the new golden rule
you got Cadillac cool
yeah you're nobodies fool
but your own.
You know all the B-sides
you know where truth lies
and you sure can make it sing.
So where to begin
you're far out
you're so in
and tell me again
how it feels to be you
cause I haven't a clue
in my every day blue
sky.
It's a wonder that I
don't shrivel and die
under the wasted weight
of my life.

SELFLESS

Delusion is your mocha-latte
you drink one every day
and I think it's fair to say
you like yours
  scalding hot
sure it hits the spot
right down where you got
nothing left to lose
just a pair of worn out shoes
and the stylish bluesy way
you live your life
out on the edge of a butter knife
  cool
  cruel
  and nobodies fool
nobody who'll talk at least
nobody who'll stop to feast
on the rotting corpse
  of a beast
you fed with both hands
and nobody understands
the toll your muse demands
and though it may seem kind of senseless
all you lost was someone else's
and in the end that's the kind of selfless
  sacrifice one can live with.

AND

And I
could see you
if you
weren't so lost in the blue
sky writing
with a sharpie pen
it ain't enough to get you high
cause you know it's true
it ain't enough for you to die
you've got to mean it too.

And you
could see me
if you
had eyes bluer than green
sea breezes
blowing up your skirt
dangerously high on the thigh.
The sum of your existence
and you're so much lighter than I
it makes all the difference.

STEAL

She's so strange
in that cool kind of way
with her orange sherbet sway
and her pink floral lei
but it's all grey
on canvas.

Taking a chance with
more than a glance was
a mere circumstance
she couldn't see
taking all three
and breaking a tree.
Lingering there
and taking he
was her way of drinking
her tea
whole.

It was never her goal
to shovel her coal
past the furnace
not to burn his
pride
in a dark, lurid
tide
of emotions
that bought her
every lesson
he taught her

babies breaking her
water
again.

Went back
to begin
took her bucket
of sin
and dipped her head
inn
house-cleaning
the little bitch
preening
at her puppies request
she let every guest
rip off her dress
a magnificent mess
of fine lines.

She was shaped
like/by a bottle
the kind she would throttle
down
swallow hard
and turn it around
a brown
clown
around town,
what she lost
can be found
by a pauper.

And so she is rosy
left with the clothes he
never asked to have
back.
She talks
like a gypsy
and waits
for the tips he
occasionally
slips free
from a sack.

And if she is graying
it goes without saying
the dream she is slaying
isn't real.
It's just a reflection
a dim recollection
of something
she just couldn't steal.

THE ROAD TO BOSTON

My mind was lost in the spaces
of Nebraska, corn fed, flat to
the grand expanses of God's
furrowed brow.

        There were crows
feasting happily on the cow gutted
remnants of one less promise left
to litter the puffed up zip-lock bag
of Reagan's America. The endless
tracks of the previous centuries
ingenuity walking along the hor-
izons edge, drawn on (un-)
erringly to the same old
destination.

        And Wyoming was just
a clue, the jack-booted trooper
with mirrored eyes, that played
the sun, in miniature. Proud and
arrogant, the General Patton of
Interstate 80, defiantly changing
the course of an asphalt river
steel logs rolling to a stop. His
swagger carried the rhythm of an
old steel guitar, bottle neck slide
for effect (and atmosphere.) The sharp
red land, paying witness to his
summery justice: his ruling for Tim
and I, merciful if a bit curt, and
ushered us on our way.

                    And our way
was on, over and through. When I was
four states out of Elko, I found that
I could breath again, having left
the last grain of the brown dust
of Nevada on an Island at a Lincoln
A and P.

        Yes we were happy for Chicago
we came like Bedouins, to a grand
oasis, to drink her muddy waters
to eat her windy and Jazz and blues
and blew us away again.

                    I dipped my toes
in the Mississippi, before rolling
on through Indiana, though Ohio
long before the green way of Pennsylvania
and the rakish corpses that marked
every mile.

                    By Providence I was all
but spent, my recollection of New
York, little more then a toll-way
to the Lincoln tunnel, where I emerged
newborn from my California dreaming
to a sort of East-coast reality
discussing Rock 'N' Roll philosophy
over an ale at the Bull and Finch.
We stayed in Worchester, warm within
the wrinkles of her run together
syllables, though sleep eluded me
for wondering, nor could I stay long for
wandering through Harvard yard.
In all ways I found Boston a fun little
lady, a bit worn around the edges
but alive and up for anything.

                    In truth
I left her almost as quickly as I found
her, eager to find my way back to a home
the road had all but worn away.

ANOTHER RAINY AFTERNOON

Another rainy afternoon
spring is running late
wont be here till June
and that old weather man
keeps humming the same old tune.

Another wasted working day
another day behind
got to make my pay
got to get to where I'm at
before I get me on my way.

Got to find a place to stand
remember all the words
of my favorite band
got to take whatever's left
and make it fit in my right hand.

Another winter day is through
Another couple of hours
till I'm alone with you
another winter's night
and it couldn't come to soon.

STORM WARNING

I heard a sigh upon the wind
the kind of static you could miss.
The merest wisp of something thick
the salty taste of blood or tears.
Feel the black clouds closing in
filling all the empty spaces
shaping all that is believed in
every self indulgent thought.
Better run for cover
better hide your colors
better paint your pallor
black.
Better close your shutters
and draw the blinds
Storm warning.

Don't feed the Beast he'll eat your hand
and when you're caught between his teeth.
He'll show you all that he would die for
if dying meant he could live
forever
like the tangles in your hair
like the dirt beneath your nails.
Salt of the earth
in your mud pie.
It's the mote within the eye
of the storm
that sees you clearly
for all that he could be.
He could paint a grim facade

with the colors that you bleed
Storm warning.

Don't get caught out in the rain
lest it strip you to the bone
the wind is howling, don't howl back
'less like the echo fade away
and all that's left is just
a retched beast
a pathetic feast
short and grim
and hard to please
a vision dim to comprehend
full of roots that have no head
and all abstract philosophies.
And if the sun could shine again
it could never be as bright
as it had been.
But isn't that the way it goes
and even photos tell a lie:
Storm warning.

RIVENDELL

I remember visions of Placerville
how it wondered my adolescent mind
rich green and warm in the dark
evening's smoky scented
rich with pine in hearth
of each imagined homecoming.
Highway 50
out the little diners eye
a magic trail that
led from my front door
to the snow white mountains
realm of my fantasies
come to life.

The Sierra's were my Misty Mountains
and Tahoe my Lothlorien.
And so this was surely Rivendell
The place where nothing ever changed
or died.

And surely if I were to stop
on my busy way
for a cup of
coffee
a bite to eat.
I would see that little boy I left behind
holding his grandfathers hand
and dreaming so
many,
many dreams.

They're so thick
like the smoke in the air.
I can touch it
breath it
but I can't grasp it.
The shapes are familiar
but not clear.
Real
but not substantial.

I return again
and again
and again
and so little changes
but it is all changed.
I am changed
and that little boy
nothing but a memory now
and Placerville
is nothing more than Rivendell
fading in my rear view mirror.
And he is far
far away,
with her
far away
beyond the western shore.

FOR A LIFETIME

Took your dreams on down to the corner store
to trade them in for something a little more
      flattering.
You said the seasons were all out of whack
but it was your fashion sense that's gone off track;
      what a sharp sting.

Well it's a wonder you can breath at all
yeah, it's a wonder you can stand so tall
      in the deep weeds
with all the termites living in your walls
and it's a wonder you never wander at all
      where the truth seeds.

You left an echo with your better half
you felt you needed to cross the track.
      What did you find?
And I'm sure you tell yourself that it's all fair
and I'm sure you almost believe it lying there
      in your own mind.

And the truth is we all somehow find a way
to live with ourselves and the price we pay
      for a goodtime.
But a child remembers every lonely night
with a clarity that burns hot and ever bright
      for a lifetime.

WHAT IT'S REALLY ALL ABOUT

The fat foot fitted me free
twisted like an old oak tree
like an ice cold cup of tea.
          Is it just me,
or something you said?
Something you dread?
something you like
to kick in the head
till it's all red
dead
and bled
out on the floor.
How we adore
a kind hearted whore
it's all such a bore
the way we need more
          and more.
It's what we're here for
to open the door
on all that and more
          or less
it's all such a mess
to you
in your pink party dress
          way
in that gay
kind of way
you can't seem to say
what it's really all about.

RHYMING A BROKEN NURSE

Mary had a little lamb
who's fleece was white as snow
but the snow was piling up so high
she didn't know where to go.
She stumbled all
around the town
looking for an open door
a place were she
could rest her head
or maybe make a score.
And the three little pigs
were all uptight
cause the big bad wolf was on the prowl
and she said to red
best get inside
when she heard the big man howl.
So they followed a snack
to the old candy shack
a real hip swinging hot spot
and Hansel and Gretel
were out of the kettle
showing the world what they got
and little Jack Horner
sat in the corner
with his thumb stuck up his ass
and Mary just stood there
shaking her head and said
"Oh dude, show a little class."
But he was too cool
to suffer a fool

besides what the hell did she know.
He was king of the scene
with a hand fool of beans
to make his old beanstalk grow.
He decided to show her
and made his way over
to the bar where Goldilocks sat
Said, "Hey there girl
you make my head twirl
and what do you think about that?"
But Goldie was coy
in no mood to toy
with someone so vapid and dense
truth to be told is
Goldie was holding
and was just here to meet with her fence.
So she shot him a stare
with her "Go to hell" glare
and you know that it fit him just right
and she smiled as he left
and sneered as he wept
and laughed as he slunk out of sight.
But just at that instant
in Papa Bear swept
pissed off and ready to rumble
and the truth can be told he
was looking for Goldie
and he sure wasn't looking for a tumble.
Goldilocks screamed
Big Daddy bear beamed
and made his way to the bar in a huff.
But just then the woodsman
stood up before him

and said, "I think that you've gone far enough."
Well the shit hit the fan
when the bear and the man
started brawling across the dance floor
and the cat and the fiddle
got caught in the middle
and it made for a horrible score.
So Mary and Red
grabbed Goldie and fled
and made there way to the Candlestick Maker's
and asked if he might
shed them some light
and Red, that deviant faker
said, "What a big man!
I'm such a big fan
we'd just love to take you to bed."
And so with a grin
he let the three in
as scenarios danced through his head
they left him that night
in a manner not quite
what the poor candle man had envisioned.
Tied to a chair
his house stripped and bare
his every silver spoon and dish gone.

A GOOD READ

I'm half way done—maybe more
and there's no way of getting
around it.
      Summer is all but over
gone to where spring resides
eternal, and autumn is so bitter
sweet. And only now are my ears
keen enough to hear with clarity
though my voice grows shrill and
thin of breath and my fingers
lack all dexterity.
      OK—and alright
and tearful smiles; welcome
and well met, with all enthusiasm
and resentment too. I am far from
anywhere I ever wanted to be, and
grateful to be there.
      The pages turn all
the faster as I become an easy read
but I'm still fascinated by it all
and eager to know how it all turns
out, if not a little dreadful of the
inevitable melancholy that comes when
one puts down a favorite finished
novel.

DAYS AND NIGHTS IN CARS

In the dying days of disco my friends
and I wore the plastic painted promise
of the new American middle class. Carter's
emaciated rundown tramp giving way to
Reagan's bloated ballroom whore.
Caught somewhere between the gritty
urban cool, and a hazy suburban
coma, we ruled the days and nights
from leather bucket seats, the last dying
breath of the American industrial dream.
We grooved in hard vinyl at the dawning age
of the tape cassette and MTV.
                        Up all night
and eating burritos and chicken supremes,
beer, rum, cheap wine and pot. Long hair
and short skirts, and the seemingly endless
rivers of pastel. Feathered hair and
feet light and deftly dancing through
beer-can mazes on the beach. We were
like the tide, coming and going with
rhythm but frothing and tangled with
weeds.
    Rolling through the Oakland Hills
at night, lights off and the radio on;
What a wonder we made it home at all,
if only for a short while yet. Before the
planes and cars,
        and wishes
            and stars,
came and took us all away, on roads

that spider web out like lines through
broken glass from that place and time
where we spent our days and nights
      in cars.

SOME PEOPLE

Some people can't see beyond themselves.
Some people can't fathom anything deeper
than their own shallow waters.
                        Some people
are locusts, stripping every fertile field
clean like their slick glass conscience
where nothing ever sticks. Like promises
made, or a child's tears, and on to the next
banquet.
    Some people wear cruelty like a hat
that fits so well, they forget it's even on.
They fling their barbs with absentminded
glee impaling all who get too close to the
fire.
    Some people spend the coinage of life
like a rich man, never knowing that they
are poor; poorer and poorer in fact with
each thoughtless purchase.

NEW AMERICAN BLUES (IN G)

Woke up in the morning
stuck my head outside my door
just to see if it was raining
cause I don't know how much more
of this pounding I can take
it keeps on trying to break me down.
I'm just trying to keep my head up
and keep my feet on solid ground.

Went down to the taxman
said I'm here to pay my share
he said you may have to pay a little more
cause the rich ain't paying theirs
and you know we got some bills to pay
you know those roads don't pave themselves.
Well I ain't going that way fella
y'all can let that one go to hell.

Went to see a friend of mine,
you know, just to shoot the shit
he was talking about the government
and everything wrong with it
and I just kept on nodding my head
as like the rhythm to a son,
he danced up on his pedestal
and I just smiled and sang along.

Well we got liberals on the left
and conservatives on the right
and their both yanking on the same rope
and this noose is getting tight
and I'm starting to believe
there ain't no stuffing in this bird.
Yeah the more I learn about it
the more I find it all a bit absurd.

And their singing Yankee Doodle
as they march us off to war
and they'll label you a traitor
if you dare to ask what for.
If you want to fight for freedom
you may have to do without.
All you need to know they'll tell you
and that's what it's all about.

And they scream like chicken little
and we're pulling out our hair
and their filling us with every
kind of crazy cooked up fear.
But the only ones that scares me
are the ones telling me "Be afraid."
Seems like things were so much safer
When I knew the man was getting laid.

Still we're buying up their oil
and we're using all their drugs
giving all our hard earned cash
to these greedy corporate thugs,
cause I need brand new Hummer
and I need my MTV.

I need a camera in my cell phone
one that plays my MP3's.

They'll tell you who to marry
and where to buy your pills
as they legislate morality
tell you how to get your thrills.
Nothing too obscene now
we got to think about the kids.
don't get caught with nothing
Jesus and your government forbids.

Well it's clearly all passé
this tired old democracy
time to dump the bill of rights
and build a new theocracy
the answers are so easy
when questions aren't allowed.
Death to the individual
Better blend in with the crowd.

September 11th
the new independence day,
From Pyongyang to old Tehran
let's blow them all away.
We'll bring democracy to the world
one bomb at a time
or maybe we'll just walk away
if all that's taking to much time.

Any way you slice it
it's good to be the king, right?
Cause the peasants wont revolt
if their fed, and touched in tight
they say, outside a storm is brewing
but the levees, they should hold.
Well I think that I'll just get off now
this nag is tired, beat and old.

THE CRADLE IS BROKEN

The cradle is broken and bent
left here barren by decades of tyranny
open to the crushing weight, come suddenly
the fierce liberty of the corporate being.
And so Eden dies, slowly and grey
that she might shed her blood for commerce
thick, black and crude as any man's heart
who knows no song but greed
        nor justice that must surely come.

LITTLE GIRL

Hey there little girl of mine
how you feeling there tonight
wrapped up in your solitude
and you know that it ain't right
for someone so young as you
to always look so down
I keep looking for that happy child
beneath your practiced frown.

Little girl don't walk away
when I'm trying to understand
all the things your going through;
I'm doing the best I can.
Little girl don't look away
when I trying to talk to you
I know that life seems hard sometime
but I can help you see it through.

And in the end you know I wish
your every dream come true
Cause when it's all said and done
there's nothing I wouldn't do
for you.

CONTRARY

Such a big little man
give yourself a hand
Yeah you're your biggest fan.
You're so in
you can barley stand it
and I really got to hand it
to you
you're so new
honest and true
blue
up on who's who
and in with a cool crew
and I'll bet you
eat your stew
with a fork.

You ain't like those parrots
stuck eating carrots
and broth
cause you're cut
from a different cloth
all artsy and goth
cutting a swath
through the thin
pale skin
of societies bargain
bin
closet of sin
and contradiction.

And you wear contrary
like a sharp new
hairdo
is it fair to
compare you
to those who
have dared to
see something more through
the stew
than the meat?

You got Voodoo?
Yeah sure you do
you're so new
and improved
Mr. B side
take pride
in your rough hide
or the grand wide
feel
of your narrow mind.
Yeah you're the kind
that can always find
the other side
of the bowl.

But here is a clue
I was just like you
so edgy and cool
that I couldn't see through
my own bullshit.
Cause it's a lame bit
to constantly sit

on the other side
of everybody else's
table.

NO PLACE TO MAKE YOUR BED

One step over the line again
and one step back from the edge
stuck in the middle of no way back
is no place to make your bed.
And what is in your little head
is often better off said than done
some things are better off fed to one
with a stronger set of teeth.

You got eyes of the bluest kind
no room for hazel there
no reason for reasons knowing
got no ribbons in your hair
and you barely even care
for all the places you dare to go
and all the faces you care to show
are reflections of nothing at all.

SHE IS

She rises like heat
the rippled illusions
running colors joined
in fleeting instances
thinning lines
disintegrate.

She sees like lizards
randomly
and blinking out of sync
a strange rhythm
all drum beat
and no bass.

She feels like smoke
fills like space
between the cracks
living on
in noises blind
indifference.

She hears like hands
rough textures
hang nailed to the wall
all wires
cable on loose
interpretations.

She talks like me
foreign tone deaf
in the eyes of the
familiar songs
reminiscent of memories
that never were.

STEWING

You say I
wince at her
pain passing to the other
defiant laughing me
to anger your
scolding her
glaring at me
to yell at the other
screaming at her
scowling at you
hurt by me
and also at her
and the other
who NO'ing you
and I
and her
separately
stewing together.

JUNK

She travels down her avenues
candied syrup on parade
blue black
the dim track
of her soft attack
and it takes her back
to a better place
she never even knew.

She is thicker
than the red river
that carries her
into every distant corner.
The garbage
rising with the tide
and baking in the public
sunlight
strips away all
illusion
leaving only
hollowed out windows
of her empty
house.

HATE

It goes deep
root twisting
dug in and
pushing earth aside
stretched out and coarse
below skin feeding
green intrusive veins
arteries of intolerance
highways of narrow passage
weedish and
base like gospel
a white stone hand
that reaching ever out
and clinging scars
heavy and marring
every painted surface.

OKTOBERFEST

I caught the train in Nuremberg
and read that (b)rail all the way
to Munich,
October of 87
and free for a bit,
yes free
from the last days of the cold war
      just for a bit.
I strolled along the avenues
from the station
to the fairgrounds
a buzzing hive of old cliché's
and new world opportunists
all dressed up in the slick
immediate style
of corporate commercial cool.

I strolled along like a legionnaire
weaving from one pavilion
to the next
      and the next
          and the next
and with pint in hand
      and schnapps
and wine
      and cheese
and brawts
      and worse
and all other things most hun
      most hun indeed.

And how that fall day
wore like summer
warm, lazy and long.

There was no room at the inn
so I slept that night
with the bulk of my generation
in the grand halls and corners
of the Munich train station.
A sea of European youth
seasoned lightly
by the occasional American
            such as I.

There were German bands
with American voices and guitars
and a thousand little Madonna's
            circa 1984
and even the occasional MJ
nice cars and silly haircuts
spoken English
both broken and whole
mingled with the German,
Chinese, French and Spanish;
(it was not unlike being in San Francisco)

At the far end of the festivities
there was a grand white building
all Greek pillared and fancy
marbled pretense.
I ate lunch in the shadow of Athena
her wisdom glaring down
on my crude American
            gall.

I arrived "home" a day later
waking at the Bamberg station
no recollection of leaving Munich
nor having made
the necessary transfer at
Nuremberg.

PERHAPS A MAN

Perhaps he is a man of sorrows
constant or otherwise
like some character
from the grapes of wrath
born of wide brown sky.
Or maybe he's all Dickens
bent down and broken
under a mountain of coal
grey black, down to his soul
and lungs full of soot
a new world martyr
a real working class hero
and John said,
"That's something to be."
Maybe he's every man
or no man at all,
maybe he's a boy
who never really grew up.

GREEK WOMEN

Circe

She's not exactly from their tribe
she's got cold metal in her eyes
cruel intensions in her thighs
and fingers painted red
well fed
and well bred
and I've heard it said
she gives good head
just ask the mindless men
fast asleep in her garden
in dreamless bliss
how they must miss
their dear high priestess
her every kiss
   a blessing
on her knees confessing
    their sin
and all the while undressing
    their skin
in truth as pink as hers
and they call that a curse
and know her for the villain
   she must surely be.

Medea

And this is me?
Cruel edge in my hand
and in my laughing
crying voice
and the little ones
that echo
      echo
        echo.

And this is me?
author to this tragic writ
returned your gift
ten fold
and bold like you
you hero you.

And this is me?
fatherless for you
and an immigrant too
nationless
and childless
and all
for love of you?

And this is me?

Persephone

Is it strange that the world
should grieve her absence so
and die white
and chilled to grey
land withered for
her absent joy.

She who
but for six seeds
would flower
all year long
and know only a child's joy.
But alas
to a cruel union
keep
this maid must
annual cycle go
and wear her
burdened ring
of gold.

And those who sleep
where her feet are pale
call her queen
and pray
for winters end.

Helen

And seeing her
Paris loved her
more than honor
king or country
and as reward
for a bold opinion
was given such a prize.

And Menelaus
seeing she was gone
was wounded to heart
(or at least where he kept it)
and was enraged
and filled with shame
for losing such a prize.

And Agamemnon
rattled his sword
and shield
and drew banners
into ranks and mast
and set them sail
to retrieve such a prize.

And Hector ended Patroclus
and Achilles ended he
and Paris he in turn
and they and others
rank on rank
bravely ended
in the name of such a prize.

But like her mother
to the swan
she was to all
but a prop
"Immortal beauty,"
that summed her up
and made her such a prize.

AVILA BEACH

Sunny calm
and lazy days
red trimmed ways
your weekend stays
      back home.
There will ever roam
the child in your eyes
in the white blue skies
and out for a bite
out by the sea side
      shopping
and restaurant hopping
summer sun stopping
by to say hello
and let you know
that when you go
a part of you never leaves
but lingers there
free of care,
in your home
      away from home.

THE GAME

You like to play the game
but more than that
you want to be the game
be in the game
learn its language
know its way
you want to live it
breath it
bleed it
and wear it
like fashion
you'll never cash in
yeah
you just let it
ride.

MAYBE W

Maybe you're not evil
Maybe you're really a nice guy
Maybe you're a real hoot
        at mixers and such
Maybe you do believe in god
        and destiny
        and all
Maybe you really believe your answering
        gods call
Maybe you're fun
        a blast to be around
Maybe you were scared
        when the towers came down
        (like the rest of us)
Maybe you're not a shill of big
        corporate oil
        or pharmaceutical companies
Maybe you're not a part of the
        Military-Industrial Complex
Maybe you're not a pawn of fat cat fucks
        sitting in darkened rooms
        selling us all
        like stocks and bonds
        like bullets and bombs
        like red heads and blonds
Maybe you didn't
        just steal your way in
Maybe you won't
        try to do it again

Maybe you aren't simply
        dumb as a rock
Maybe someone
        should be sucking your cock
Maybe this isn't just
        all about your dad
        or how they tried to kill him
        or his good Saudi friends
Maybe you're not just a spoiled rich brat
        clueless and lost
        trying desperately to stay afloat
        while New Orleans drowns
Maybe you're just the Warren G. Harding
        of our generation
Maybe you're just the wake up call
        we all have needed
Maybe you aren't a shallow
        and cruel
        money grubbing
        mean hearted
        prick
Maybe
        but that doesn't make you
        any less wrong.

UN-IAMBIC PENTAMETER

I pedestrian armature
(all un-iambic pentameter)
to ice in the tray
of a heavy lidded hipster you
arched brow goateed spectacle
slander my peg-foot awkward phrasing.
Musings of a semi-conscious mind
won't snug in your boots
but meander crocked offerings
all Dickenson crude
by your Ginsberg critique
all the while
edit heavy handed quills
pissing in the (ex-)stream
bleed your tortured thoughts
before they can even breath.

BUTTERFLY

Winter long lay kyton in your bed
hours measure strands wrapping paper thin
lost in layers crossed and all stitched in
time will come and thaw the frigid
rest, in blooming season wake
fresh in May's dawn, a mind new
      in knowing spring.

YOU AND I

You say
and I laugh a little
cause I think
but you smile and giggle
cause you know
and I sigh as usual
and I grin
but you whisper something
and you frown
so I come closer to you
and I say
and you smile again.

CASSIE SAY

Cassie say
"My wings are almost dry now,"
moisture rising to her lips
      it's in her hips
      she quips,
"Spin me vinyl halo plattered
cello moans,
      viola
      slipping through.
Credit me one liner notes
between grooved concentric prayers.
Say me you and never ending
      and ever ending
living, dieing, born a(K)new."

FACE IN BLACK INK & PENCIL

From inner darkness
risen porcelain pale
and wide eyed
before the glaring
      bearing
          and exposed
nerve endings
      beginnings
and the spaces in-between
beat, beat, beat
heart quivers lashes
long and drawn
      up
short and turned
      down
to full lips
slightly parted
perhaps to kiss
      or
perhaps to speak
a whispered truth
that wont betray
what philosophies
reside in
such perfect brows.

RIGHT NOW

She is nearly perfect
        right now
taking every breath
with unpolluted lungs
free of societies carcinogens
the yellow brown smog
that dulls the worlds colors
and makes us slowly grey.
She sees no grime
        nor wear
her eyes are open
as only a child's can be.
She does not hate
        nor fear
        nor jade.
She will not devalue
        detract
        or despair.
She is whole
as only a child can be.
She is fresh
like spring after rain.
My precious rose,
the world must change us all
but she is nearly perfect
        right now.

TOWNCAR

A flesh of light
as a breeze
e Male man
in drag
ing your feet
deep under
ground to bits
of time.
      Ex Watch
men at workload
ing up towncar
crash course
ing through vain
regard fore-
      thought.

A BLUE MONDAY

I know you
Ok I do.

I do
know you
it's true
though I haven't a clue
how you
know who
ever got through
to you.

You know who
must have flew
through
your view;

Whew
it makes me stew
to think of you
and you
know who
and the rest of the crew
wasting a blue
Monday away.

SELF-INDULGENT

Why am I
sitting here
writing
        writing
                writing
        today

why must I bleed
my every
stray
        stray
        stray
        thought

a dalliance
and self-indulgent shit

why can't I stop
my fingers
be still
        be still
        be still
        and rest

and remembering
every syllable
uttered
        uttered
        uttered
        in me

finds purchase
here black on white
written
  written
  written
  out of me

DROP

Drop
splatter thin
coalesce

Drop
beat, beat
me heart
and lungs
of air

Drop, drop
rhythm
pulling down
running down
like candle wax

Drop
in and over
and down the
sides

Drop, drop
painted thick
and sticky
red to brown
to rust

Drop, Drop
in constellation
and oracle
me living
grey

Drop
by drop
pale before
symphonies
grim and true
to the last

Drop

APEX BEFORE THE FALL

We stand apex
before the fall
bees (in) four by four
parading S U V
indulgence
the last march
of the American dream.

We come
black clip-on tied
ready for the feast
eager to dine
on the crumbs of those
new age Robber Red Barrens
obese kitties in the pallor
skimming the cream
and leaving the dream.

and there ain't no
knickerbocker
out on the horizon
no Teddy bear to save us now
not this time.
We are roman before the Hun
and he is red
in righteous hate.

We are pawns, we bitches we
of big (bad) business men
momentary CEOs
who rape tomorrow
behind the board room doors.
On our knees
before their erect
and glossy towered manhood
already limp and
spent
before the desolate
horizon.

NICKEL

I feel nickel
in a world of dimes
half valued
in a bloated kind of way
and though I'm but a fifth
of a quarter
and short by comparison
I still feel thicker
buy just a bit.

PAINLESS DAYS GONE BY

Her blood is thin and cut with poison
a malignancy that veins its way
down every dark and twisted artery
        down her every avenue.

And when the devils blackened seed
finds purchase in her sacred soil
she screams her prayers in tortured silence
        in heavy tortured silence.

Exhaling through her bloodshot eyes
blistered red, worn and tired
and torn apart like paper sheets
        like the ripping of paper sheets.

She yields then to the dark embrace
in the fevered trance she tears a bit
and dreams of days now long gone by
        of painless days now long gone by.

THE CAFE

He was 19 and bored
sitting on the edge of forever
with a pocket full of presidents,
some car keys
and a few old concert
ticket stubs.

And she smiled at him
and said,
"I could ride this train
to some day."
But he was already there

in the narrow of the road
where the scenery
closes in
in that country where
he could almost touch it,
almost.

And his eyes were like
traveling salesmen
in aimless pursuit of destinies
ripped from the backs
of middleclass housewives
cooked up
and served with a greasy spoon.

And the glass eyed sheriff
dining on half cooked eggs
rattled his keys
at girls
who paraded their curves
down whiskey streets
in heels.

And the tranny drank
his/her
coffee both with
cream and sugar,
and swallowed his/herself
in anguished protests
before the petulant
cook
who greased every mouth
that assed their way
up to his long
thin table.

And when she went
to return
a portion of her meal
he took his leave
with a fresh new flower
who just yesterday
had taken to the road,
and left her there
in the dusty air
filled with old jukebox tunes

BEFORE YOUR CROOKED CROSS

You've got to be
the thickest ghost
I've ever seen
it's mean
and obscene
to see
all the shit you put in
the minds your children
fill them up to the rim
        with your hate.

How does the world
make such creatures as you
vile little maggots who
are more than happy to chew
on the philosophies of utter
asses as Pierce and Hitler
or the sermons Butler
what a dumb mother fucker
        you are.

But as you kneel
before your crooked cross
and teach your young
of sacrifice and loss
before you read to them
from the Turner diaries
or tell them of Waco
and the Ruby Hill tragedies

be sure to mention
Okalahoma City
and the 19 children
brought low without pity
be sure they know
what a gutless prick
        you really are.

IS WRITTEN

i was pour
in my Hat 4
E.E. Cummings

All bent
on easy Cum
Ming
and going verse
that altered E-
go's shirt(less)
tied
about a
little, big town.

ONE SYLLABLE

To write a poem
with but words
that have one beat
no two
    three
      or four
is more hard than
one might think.
Though in the end
it may sound a bit
like fluff,
      it won't sit
fat on a man's thick
tongue.

HAIKU FOR TWO

Two, my precious gems
they products of our loving union
Carry me anon

BROADWAY

City street lights
sharply color midnight
cruel and hip
like some independent
urban flick
or that kind of dingy
TV police show
where every shade
filters in kind.

The dingy air
thick with smokes
(legal and otherwise)
is suddenly torn
by the predatory growl
of a Harley Davidson motorcycle
doing its best
to eat everything else
a sound course
for such a greedy
beast

and the barkers
bite
your ears
like pit bulls
hungry for your
silver and green.
Thirsty under neon
HEAT
and X's everywhere.

And clear-heeled dancers
stand idle
in the allies
off the poles
and off their laps
for a break
giving head
to their cancer
styx.

And street corner
ingenuous
and the after dark
Marquis de-Sades
find free market love
in momentary unions
in hotel rooms
and Toyota Corollas.

And yesterdays heroes
find warmth
in the news of the day
down toilet allies
or dead end ways
where they were chased
from sleeping
in public parks.

BI-POLAR

I think I might be
schizophrenic
cause I don't right
like me
even when I do
it's wrong or left
or it's a me in pieces
with filed down edges
and make a puzzle
of that
I dare you.
Go ahead
and put it in your hat
like the feather
of some obscure parrot
who's voice is always
changing
       ChanGing
             cHANgING.

It is strange though
I feel in(di)visable
even odd in a way
that is all together
(whole) and optical.

And it's just that kind
of (double s)peak
that makes you
wonder what I'm at.

HAIKU FOR SAM

Got stung one day at
the Renaissance Faire by an
un-period bee.

DIGITAL TESTIMONY

I'm not always
poetically correct
I've been known to beat
a word or two behind the rhythm
if I happen to think
it will make my point.

There's not always a reason
to nature of my rhyme
though I rhyme my reasons well
from time to time
I tend to approach it all
with a sort of sublime
piece of mind.

Sure I may walk
a syllable
or tow
down a kittycat walk
both in the same damn shoe
but it's just cause my fashion
sometimes fashions
that way.

Ok, Ok
so it's not so much "STYLE"
as it is style
but it takes all the guile
I can muster

to pass on to you
these cerebral extractions
hunted and pecked
out in fractured line
after line
of digital testimony.

FEVER

In fitful sleep
she is assaulted by fever
a malignant cancer
that spreads unchecked
eating her slowly
away.

And she shrugged
suddenly
violently awake
and moved
in hot rigid slides
against countless
cold hard surfaces.
Her face newly lined
by cracks that ran
out like lightning
dancing across the
midnight sky
but dark
and dry as dust.

She shutters
like jello
shutters
shutters
shutters
racked by hard vibrations
that set her waters

and running
running
running
for dry land
and nothing stands
before them.

She burns with fevers
smoke
and steam
vomits heat
and red hot bile
or coughs dry fits
ash grey
and dirty snow
that eats the air
the beast
the fields alike.

And with twisted
smoking fingers
she scratches her skin
so raw in places
that the scars
may never heal.

In her fevered wrath
she screams and howls
and throws her tears
like diamond slivers
racing in the arms
of frantic
winds

that tear her
edges down.

And if her seas
rise up
to swallow her face
and her body
is tortured
until it is utterly
unrecognizable
will we learn
how to love her then?
Or simply be washed away
with the storm.

CASSIE TOO

Cassie stands out
in a way that
fits right in
spreads her dirty wing
adjusts her smoky ring
and smiles
the bartender
for another round.

She likes to sit
and drink her
whisky sour
and tarts
just a little
for the boys
at the far end of the bar.

She tries hard not to laugh
at the enthusiastic salesman
to her right
mustering all
his comb-over cool
as he lobs his pitches
he's throwing heat
trying hard
to close her deal.

But her supply is low
and tonight
demand is high

cause the currency
is faith
and tonight
it's in abundance.

And she sits and drinks
and watches all
the boys and girls
how they dance
or how they dance
about
with smiles
and laughing eyes
and shy demure
and gentle touching
(just his arm)
and flutter blinking coy
and winking charm
and smug over confident
and insecure sexuality
and eyes
and eyes
and eyes.

One last swig
an oral punctuation
and she flows off her seat
like water
struts a tempo
dark and heavenly
as she
rhythms her way
to the stage.

The drummer catches beat
and the band climbs aboard
and she dons
an old guitar
wears it
like a crucifix.
Closes her eyes
and gives the mic a kiss
(almost.)

And she sings in strange
familiar dialects
of secrets
everybody knows
and they sing along
but she isn't fooled
cause she can see
right through you.

MOBILE

Sometimes
you just have to
pen it out
let these little beasts
grow as they would.
Let them
breath me swollen
thoughts
bursting
at the seams
like ecstasy
like chocolate
cream filled Easter
on Christmas
evening news
and olds
mobile
like my head
it all keeps
coming around.

MOJAVE HIGHWAY

He rips through
this desolate land
wide-eyed and alive
at last
at last
free in his vintage
cobalt blue
Chevy El Dorado.
A sort of highway gladiator
out of the ring
and free
for the first
time.

He hums along
to some old
familiar tune
that he really can't remember
and "When that old song plays,"
it really is
"more than a feeling"
it's inside him
like DNA.

And the desert wind
batters what's left
of his failing hair
and wrinkled eyes
and carries the dry
hard promise

of a new tomorrow
pulled red hot
and searing
from this crucible
highway
that rivers its way
on through
the American landscape
portrait
on its way
to a brighter
set of days.

AMEND THIS

Young couple walking
  hand in hand
old couple watching
  don't understand.
They see a difference
  in their reflection
think their left is right
  their right is left and
we got to see beyond
  the labels
beyond the fairy tales
  and the fables.

Must we draw lines
  in the sand?
Isolate the things
  we don't understand?
Must people always be
  in fear
of the things that they perceive
  as odd or queer
see it all as deviant,
  strange or lame
but in the end
  I think it's all the same.

X and Y
         OR X AND X
             OR Y and Y
we all have salt
         in the tears we cry

that burns in wounds
         inflicted by
the intolerance
         in hateful eyes.
And what if all
         the world were grey
no black or white
         no straight or gay
and love was celebrated
         not condemned
by narrow points of view
         (or religious Acumens)

Maybe then God
         might finally recognize Us.

FASHION TRENDS

And God said,
"Are you really going to wear that?"
and I said,
"Why the hell not!"
and he said,
"Exactly"
and I didn't understand.

CHICAGO BY TRAIN

I blew into Chicago
breezy and cool
like every other
wind swept
adolescent train hopper
wide eyed
and slightly left
of sober.

I strolled an
unremembered distance
down city streets
and vast wide ways
blown impossibly clean
by the constant
breath
of Lake Michigan
that howled
in my ears
like jazz.

I ate alone
outside some pizza joint
some deep-dish water
kind of pizza joint
and watched
as business people
rivers flowed
this way
       and that
            and that

pausing for
red damn temporaries
and off again
with the green
flow.

I watched some queen
of the avenues
as she and her
curly headed beast
made decadent way
down oblivious sidewalks
her beast sniffing
every passing foot
while she
just sniffed
the sky.

And I caught a cab
at the corner
of I don't care
and didn't notice
anyway
and faired
on down to the
Sears Tower.

And I just stood there
for a moment
shrinking
in a shadow
lighter
than the black

on black
of that comically
overstated tower.

I shared an elevator ride
with a small nation
strangers
that were oddly familiar
and similar
to every other
stranger I know
which is to say
all together
foreign.

I made my way
to the observation deck
and found a tight spot
between
a nice bland family
from somewhere
in the middle
and
two goth chick
pretend lesbians
performing for
horny lunch-break
business men
and elevated
security guards.

And as I looked
across
the flat of Illinois
to the slightly different
promise of Ohio,
I wondered then
of Pennsylvania
or perhaps
the shores of
Michigan?

EN' VOGUE

Oh I don't
know
   no
   no
you don't
feel it in your
chess master
puppets
on strings
made of cheese
and smile
for the camera
for your close
up
  down
    and all
  around
the Rosie
(hands in her)
pocket
full of
pose(she)
upside down
in the eye that
shutter
    shutter
        shutters
and winks ever
and always
at the strangeness

of beauty
emaciated
    dying
en' vogue.

PHOTOGRAPHS

Petrified moments
of grace
or happy
sad
gloomy
glad
gathered
loss
(or lost)
in color
or
black and white
or countless shades
of gray
that yellow withered
weathered
and paled by
time

still
what stories
these
old photographs
tale

PYRITE

Once
when I was young
and newly arrived
in house of men
I lost me
in the cruel maze
of adolescence
grasping for titles
only kings
and queens
may bestow.
But bereft
of any real-estate
I was homeless
in the suburbs of
click.fashion.academia

And so
I adorned myself
in shame
and walked on
crooked feet
all for the amusement
of others
who's riches
were as pyrite
as my own
who's banner
dragons
where nothing more

than chameleons
painted thin
on pretense
and hallow-noted voices
light as smoke
and baseless.

But in these crimes
I company well
with generations
fore
and aft
for we all
sin a little
against our own
better judgment.

FOOTWHERE

Oh I have nicer shoes—sure
but what's the point
when the miles fall away
so easily.

B4

B4
Before me
It'll be four wins today.
Bingo!

FREE-MARKET

You think that I
have no teeth
just because I
wave my peace
in front
of your face.

Well I'll tell you
it's not true
you see I just
don't have a
taste for you
or your
particular brand
name violence.

I'm handicapped
you see
blind to your
marketing scheme
to your
new world order dream
I guess I didn't
get the memo.

Now don't get me wrong
I am more than willing
to do battle
on evil men
in the name of

God
and the dispossessed.
I just don't think
the whores that
fill your suit
are the type
to wear that dress.

I guess
in the end
I just don't care
about your
profits
in or out
of the margin,
cause it ain't like I'm
gonna cash that check
right?
And it ain't
a free market
when someone's
holding a gun.

I BELIEVE

I believe in God
     but not so much his religions
I believe in Jesus
     and Mohamed and Buda too
I believe in lower taxes
     starting with the poor
I believe in less government spending
     especially on guns
I believe that equal rights
     should mean equal opportunity
I believe that with great power
     comes great responsibility
I believe that you could say as much
     about the possession of greater wealth
I believe when it comes to the government
     less is nearly always better
But I also believe that with greedy corporations
     we should watch their every move
I believe that men corrupt the system
     not the other way around
        and that corruptible men
     are drawn to power
I don't believe there were any
     weapons of mass destruction
I believe that the idiots in charge
     believed there were
I don't, however, believe they ever
     thought they were ever any threat.
I believe that it is harder to be the hero
     than to play the villains

I believe it is a traitorous thing
        to hold us down to enemies standards
                just to justify our own criminal
                        behavior
I believe that moral values
        must change with society
I believe that it is my job as a parent
        to teach those morals to my children
I don't believe in labels
        I just believe in people
I believe in the greatness of America
        but believe that we can do better

NOW

Now is
an illusion
created
as the future
falls
into
the past.

TEMPORARY RELIGIONS
(OF A PERMANENT GOD)

God is flexible
define him
how you like
she doesn't really care.
Chop him
into little pieces
or swallow her
whole.

Hear him
through
the prophets words
or the caterwaul
call
of charlatans.

See her
forming
formed
in magic
or shaped
by the hard
cold lines
of science.

Feel him
warm
in a saviors touch
or cold
bitten cruel
by the devils lash.

Taste him
bitter/sweet
irrelevant.

Her scent
will fill your head
auras revelating
in your mind.

Know him
for the you
she is.

Temporary Religions
(of a permanent God)
come and go
with their scrapbook
enlightenment,
but faith
is everlasting.

MOVE

Tell me again
how it is
you move
without wheels
without gears
or any kind
of machinery?

You got some
mystic motivation
some divine
mobilization
or are you
just sliding along
in the wake
of someone else's
passage?

POETIC METHOD

Method OK(you got to get with the program)as written

    //declare your variables up front

    Love
    Lust
    Passion
    Desire
    Exhaustion
    Sex
    Envy
    Life
    Death
    Soul

    If Love = Lust then
            do while Desire > Exhaustion
                        Sex
    else if Love = Passion
            do while life > Death
                        Love
    else
            Life = Envy

    return Soul

End Method

BRIGHT RED KNICKERS

The sky fell without warning
and fathered such chaos
that rivers rolling under
flat wide ways steep tilted
in avalanche approach
roared porcelain sharp
with incisor relevance
that entered like ghosts
the deaf pearl ears
of prophecies prostitutes
as they washed their bright
      red knickers clean.

YOU ARE NOT FROM OUR TRIBE

You wear the wisdom of others
in the hollow hope that it might
one day make you seem less shallow
in the eyes of deeper minds.

You lurk in digital shadows
filling you're empty MindSpace
with visions of an alien make.

You are not from our tribe
you are a descendant of poachers
a mere consumer amongst the
merchants of rhythm and verse.

THE SOUND OF ABSENCE

A Monday night
8th of December
1980, I remember it well.
It was my favorite time of year
and I was happy and alive
perhaps a bit to juvenile
for my nearly 15 years
basking in the multicolored glow
of our family Christmas tree
my old stocking with the Rudolph
red nosed Santa pin on it
and the Dolphins in battle
with some team I don't remember.
Howard Cosell's voice was
doing summersaults in my head
meandering through holly visions
all green and red and gold.

That's when I heard them say
that you'd been shot, in New York
in front of your home

And then everything stopped
And I thought "That can't be right."
and they said you were gone
and I thought "No, that can't be right."

And then—

Nothing, I did not cry, move, breathe
the world became surreal to me
eerily silent
and in that silence I heard
the hollow sound of absence.

I had never really lost anyone before
no one that I felt so connected to
(and I didn't even know you)
"Nobody told me there'd be days like these,"
"strange day's indeed."

LIKE RAVENS DO

She bleeds like ravens do
she sings like them too
harsh and challenging
channeling
and what can it bring
to the cold ears of a
prophet.
It's a little off topic
cause you know she's got it
bad
every thought she had
indifferent good or bad
was dark blue, drunk and mad
as a lark
screaming in the dark
"Die"
"Die"
"Die"
You black pearls of I
tortured starless sky
of my broken minds eye
why
oh tell me will you
why
do all blades dull
before my concrete
veins
run black
like ravens do.

SACRED DIRT

I dreamt of red lies on black
sack cloth promontories
that open up all wide mouthed
before a gapping chasm of lilies.
The air took inventory of
such scattered weeds as purchased
time in the house of sacred dirt.
it was a beggars field to be sure
       fertile in conflicting colors.

ONE LAST KISS BEFORE SHE LEFT

And she thought
"I'd rather drink your violence
then sit inside my solitude
and listen to the aching
of my soul,"
and she breathed in
more pollution
and spun herself
one last time
one last kiss
before she left.

But she was once
a happy child,
Momma's little girl
her daddies
pride and joy.
But pride became
a withered beast
joy up and left her
for the coast
and left behind
that little girl
with one last kiss
before she left.

And she just couldn't
seem to make it home
even when it found her.
For her demons

were too strong it seems
for all her loved ones
hopes and dreams.
She just couldn't
find a way away
from one last kiss
before she left.

And now she's gone
and guilt remains
a hurt that may never
truly heal
and how they wish
if for nothing else
but for one last kiss
before she left.

PEWTER

She dreamed me
a man of silver prize
but I felt all pewter
before her diamond eyes.

EDINBURGH

I took a plane
to Edinburgh
newly arrived from
the modern antiquity
of London town.
I climbed
a royal carriage way
that ascend
wide and flat
before the ancient face
of that stately house
of iron, mortar and stone
home of Mary's
and Kings of many names.

Up the serpentine way
of Edinburgh castle
that stony way
that led so serendipitously
from the murderous womb
of her portcullis
past the once grim
shops and homes
now quaint
and long bereft of their
medieval purpose
on to the castle proper
where I sat
like some new world raven
over Scotland's heart.

Peering out and over
fair Edinburgh
past a quiet park
to the majesty
of princes street
where old brown pubs
and warm lit tavern windows
played host to alien ventures
like Burger King
and Pizza Hut.

I took a train
from Edinburgh
through the Scottish
countryside
green
like no other green
not the green of California
which is yellow gold
like sunlight.
Not the green of
F. Scots Fitzgerald
or the blue green, green
of Kentucky grass
but green
that green
that only grows in Scotland
and I suppose
in Ireland too.

Later I returned
to Edinburgh
from adventures
in the frozen north
and walked along
her happy ways
and filled my lungs
with her frigid warmth
and mine eyes
her timeless grace.

I left that night
from Edinburgh
and though never
have I returned.
I still know
and love her well
in my own
American way

WE RIVER DEEPLY NOW

We river deeply now
thawed from snows
packed high
in lofty aeries.

We came
down
drop
by
drop
and collected
in rivulets
crawling to
thin line
to thick and
ever thicker.

We randomed
at first
slowly
brought together
by the shear act
of living
and time's fostered
familiarity.

When first we streamed
we walked unsure
this way
and that
but ever together
till the conduit
came rushing down
and when those
winding ways
dropped occasionally
shear
and sudden
we leapt together
our falls
roaring down
to the valley floor
and crashed
in silver fired foam
misting out
and on again.

And now
we are a mighty
and true momentum
that rain
may only swell.

For our overflowing
has fed the earth
and left seeds
of precious
unions.

WRITTEN

I was written
in blood red ink
by carotid
choking
thin sheeted creatures
who give
their crooked shapes
away
with their stutter
shutter
stop-action
choreography.

They'd stone me
beggar transparent
shear
and peer
me through
my muddy waters
just to glimpse
some sense of I
or swallow
eyelids
of wayward me
lost on roads
of indefinable
destination.

OUR VAN GOUGH SOULS

With a
  ViViD
    clarity
      of
  COLOR
giv
   i
     n
    g a sense of
M
  o
   t
   i
     o
      n
(e)
  m
   o
  t
   i
     o
       n   s

living in
     still life
  and
breathing
    smelling
      tasting
  the

tortured
    voices
of our
    Van Gough
souls.

WEAPON SMYTH

I could spit
a thousand words
just fling them out
like daggers.
Sink them each
like hungry beasts
feasting on the flesh
of all I loath.

I could father
an army of verse
legion
upon
legion
of syllables
all olive drab
and jackbooted
graceful killers
they.

I could forge
finely crafted phases
all diamond edged
and sharp
as glass
and smooth
like water
running.

I could drop
atomic syllables
like
"melodramatic moron"
and wipe out
whole cities of
cancerous
offenses.

But in the end
with power
must come
responsibility
and selfish hates
must never
be given their
reign.

THE DANCE

The eyes
of my adversary
seem small and narrow,
more like the eyes
of terrier
trying to wear
his best
pit-bull contact
lenses.

He thinks
he knows me
has me
figured out
he reaches across
the dusty distance
between us
to extended
a dirty white
idea.

His best guess
tumbles
red over
      thread
         over red
his arching thought
aimly seeking
the other side
of its intended
goal

the one
farthest from my reach
"what brilliance"
he muses
from the edge of his
rubber pedestal

till he recons
the red glint
in my eye.

Mistake!

Too late,
I move suddenly
instinctively
in my practiced
act of violence
a simple reaction,
from the legs
        to the hips
                to the arms
        and Contact!

Base hit.

SLEEP

He comes down
quiet, thick and
heavy like warm
almost remembered
yesteryears and
promise kept.
Makes me lungs
so thick
they strain
against
my rib-caged-bird of
a feathered bed
and steals
my expressions
in exchange
for the
shutter drawn
drawl
of drooling
child.

SLEEPING STONE

I am stone
my god
I'm stone
heart still beating
mind retreating
depleting
my sense of
now.

I am half(a)way
here
not here
or there
but lost
in the dim
hazy limbo
between
the waking
and the un-
waking

I am frightened
captive
of this
near real
nightmare
unmoving
within
the machinery
of night

I am heart
beating loud
like Bonham
and just behind
the rhythm
of my
choir

I am heavy
breathing
short
and fast
always
reaching for
the next.

I am screaming
out to you
in silence
loud
like the sound
of wind
behind
the thunder.

I am stone
my god
I'm stone
and will waking
ever come
and thaw
my frozen
soul?

ILLUSIONS

I thought love
        was magic
until I realized
magic is an illusion
and though magic
        may love create
in the end
all illusions
must dissolve
in the epic depths
of loves embrace.

IF I WERE SEVEN

If I were seven
I would be divine
but I am five
for such is the number of man
and to get to seven
you must go through six
and that's the devils realm
so best you take a hat.

LAST NIGHT'S ANGER

I.

I am the red beating stain, the
quiet fire that must not burn
moving through courses of the flesh
and aching bones in quiet tense
       and rage
            and rage
                 and rage
with black thought water marked
and razor swam through grey matter seas
and tarries there a predator
       like hunger
             like death
                 like me

II.

I can not speak calm anymore
for my tongue's fat-meated
become a trembling creature
illiterate and base, and cruel
       in every way.
I fire, fire, fire,
I eat me soul in ravenous bites
I expand at the speed of hate
these are not my eyes
they are monstrous orbs
green, brown and black
       black
          BLACK.

The world leaves trails
reminders of its persistent nature
it's unwillingness to bend
or yield and give me a moments
peace, a moments rest, a moment
without this me that is burning
like some Auschwitz Jew, like some
mangled corpse of the joy that
was me just hours ago
                just days ago
                                just a lifetime ago
I can't see my world
this one's in the way
but which was real?
and which is the fantasy
                the dream
                                the nightmare
there are no guides out here
out here everything is tangled
                trail-less
                                endless
                                        dark.
I want to come home
but I have lost my keys
my only hope lies somewhere
                in this written
                                page.

III.

I would kill this vile creature
                if it were not my heart

IV.

Is it gone now
can I breathe again,
can I see colors real
        unfiltered and clear?
is this just a trick?
        No.
I am calm after the storm
tired and salty air of spent
Happy to be anything not mad
sad to be standing in the ruins
        of me
but grateful for everything
        that's left to carry on.

QUESTION OF WIDTH?

I don't understand
the question.
Could you ask it
any differently?
Perhaps walk your phrases
wider then narrow
maybe then
I could know you
for more
then the thickness
of your nose.

THE OLD DREAM

I hare
through the forest
'neath the dark
towered pines
all about
over lost limbs
that protest
Snap!
Snap!
Snap!
and rattle
and reaching up
and draw some blood
occasionally.
Like rose redded
thorns
and berry pointed
holly leaves.

I hear them
closer now
all around
their angry prayers
moon sung
and blessed
by her
with light
enough
to find
my scent.

And green breaks
before a sudden clear
and she laughs
her silver smirks
upon my
terrored
head.

Caught here
in this ring of doom
they come
and slide
from shadowed
forest depths
and close
with cruel grim
lupine smiles.

And the leader,
silver as his
mothers crown,
steps through
the distance
menacing
and as his face
to mine
and breath...

Awaken
and in my place
that has changed
so many times
but that dream
still remains
ever the same.

HEAVY IN HERE

Ok
so my Gothic-
a friend
said "it's getting
heavy in here,
yeah the air's
so thick
like gumbo stew
easy to chew
(like you know who)
just a little racy
just a little blue
and don't make me
tell you
          again
step away
from the pen
and let your
good times
roll.

US MONET

Heartache
     and longing
expressed
    in
rhythmic
     patterned
         syllables
Most
   clearly
paint
   us
     Monet
in the minds
      eye
        of those
who read
    our souls.

SPOON-FED

You should learn
how to fill
your lungs
yourself,
break free
from that respirator
of stale
recycled
doctrine.
After all
there's more
to life
then what
you can eat
with someone else's
spoon.

LIKE DOLPHINS DO

If you could hear
like dolphins do
(through your jaw
that is)
you'd have heard
it all by now.

HAVE LIT FIRES

I have lit fires
in the wide
gray planes
just to watch them
burn.

I have sung
love songs
to the wind
too heavy
for a voice
as thin as mine
just to see
if I could stop
the rain

I have told tales
to bridge keepers
who,
trollish
as they were,
fanged me grins
wide as Kentucky
and deep
as the Frisco
Bay.

I have woven
fair deceits
in tales
as grim
as a fairies
heart
broken before
the tempest
gale.

I have spoken
secrets
to the night,
whispered truths
known only
to her
and mine muse
who smiles with eyes
that know
my soul.

BUFFALO

I was Buffalo
for a day
(but just a day)
neck high white
and chilled
to the soul
where bones
are just
an illusion.

My mind
was a murdered
thing
damp, muddy grey
like Lake Eerie
that I sea now
only blue on
maps.

And as I
stole the length
of my cigarette
in the ice cold
ambiance of
the greyhound
station,
I thought
of the warm
arms of my
childhood home

in a land called
California.

I was Buffalo
for a day
(but just a day.)

PICASSO WE

These a(R)e
      Frac-
  tured
  truths
These
  piece-
      s
  of
      me
   and
you
seg-
  re-
     gated
  philosophies
  of
the
  Picasso
  we.

JAZZ CLUB GIRL

She's the kind of girl
that could eat
blue notes for dinner
sitting in her
practiced pose
at a round
little cocktail table
head tilted
at just the right angle
for the red
netted candle
to throw
orange caresses
lovingly
at her face.

Her blood
red hair
cut like
a flappers
frames her
porcelain beauty
coal rimmed eyes
of impossible blue
taken twilight
off some long ago
sea.

She dangles one
black leather pump
ended fish net peg
over the other
and keeps time
to the angry rhythms
of a poets rant.
Her lips
that have known
the verse
of countless authors
takes smoke
from a cigarette
like it was
her lover.

And as the club
swims about her
she sits
absolutely still.
She's so perfect
at being her.

SWEET MISERY

Sweet Misery
stumbles down
the dark ally ways
looking for her angel
in Any-city America.

And she howls out
in a voice
only hounds
would care
to hear.

And she wears an
anguished face
even the
gang-bangers fear

and she aches
how she aches

Her bones
scream
trapped
under the weight
of her wasted life
as it trickles
through her
veins.

And she dies
again
there in the ally
she just falls
down and
dies,
but body
refuses
to let her
go.

And then
he's there
her angel
of death
come to give her
a few more hours
of life
and he smiles
that picket fence smile
and his soulless
eyes cruel
grey.

He's talking now
low in his
candy lying tones
she doesn't feel
as he takes
the bone and flesh
that was once
her arm
Pressure now

and she anticipates
the…

    Once
    when she was young
    sitting under
    an old elm tree
    in the golden hours
    of sunset
    her father said
    "The world is for you
    and everything in it
    so choose wisely
    my sweet Marie"

…Pinch,
and the pain
receding
and heaven sweeps
her up inside
and her head
rolls back
as she counts
every one
of her heart beats
each against
a different star
and she lives again
just rises up
and lives
but body
refuses
to let her
go.

And in the corner
of her eye
Sweet Misery sees
her devil's picket smile
and she howls
but even the hounds
refuse to hear her.

POLLOCK BEAT

S
  p
  l
   a
    t
     t
     e
      r
       e
        d lines
   de-
(syl
   lable)-
constructed
      c
     h
   a
    o
        s of the
    MIND
 takes ->
     s
   h   a
    p e
in(k) d0t
     to -> page
in a Pollock
kind of beat.
      beat.
        beat.

KAHLO EYES OF MINE

The innocence of color
    may see below
       where
       death
       eats
       down
       to
       life.

                        corpse
                 every
            from
        rises
    abundant
  life
Yet
    ViViD
  in these
Kahlo eyes of
  mine.

COMMON

He sits there
pale before
the off white walls
on a child's bed
made long ago.
The trappings
of happy days
seem to antique
within his
naked eyes.

He stands there
thin within
this widest room
at the foot of
his father bed.
Remnants of
another world
a time before him
lie all about.

And he is living
that long ago
captured in
a photograph
that is
just beyond
his grasp.
The son he lost
to the narrows

of his mind
those words
of hate
he authored
a cross he
fashioned cruelly.

And he is wishing
for that long ago
when he sat high
upon his father's back.
Long before
his own desire
betrayed his father's
moral sense;
before his own
back bent
with shame
beneath the cross
his father
gave him.

And now they lie
in different rooms
of a common hall
facing a common
fate
eaten by cancer
devoured by AIDs
Their common blood
Their common end
In the eyes of
Their common God

1 A.M. SATUDAY MORNING

Michael,
    Angelo
        and me
caught a train
        at half-past three
and railed
        roads from there
                to
        the rocky mountain
high as a kite
        and twice as wide
as it was long.
        And Mike said
this has got
        to be wrong
                these pebbles
        seem Boulder
                than dirt (or Denver)
caught under my nails.

In a coffin
        he'd sleep
                if vampires
        were cool
                anymore
or less trendy
        than a wolfman.

And Jack and Jill
  kept popping pills
    and Angelo just
  couldn't sleep.
So he handed me
  a secret to keep-
    sake,
  safe
and sound
  advice if you
    can get it
  should never
    be left
  out in the rain
right or
  wrong.

SQUID INK

I know I write
a little left
it's just I left
my pen
in my right shoe
and what's left
just doesn't seem
rite.

You see
it makes for a feather
far from my cap.

Oh well
at least I see
there's still ink
in my well
if no squid
in my sea.

DEEP

If her eyes
were any deeper
I would surely drown
for in those depths
I am ever complete
and desire
the air
of nowhere
      else.

I'VE

I've got feet
as fickle
as a summer
breeze
always blowing
here and
there
but never
far from
home.

I've a mind
that sometimes
strays a bit
through minefields
of far fetched
ideologies
or lingers
long in meadows
of abstract
philosophies.

I've a gut
that's shy
and delicate
in nature
and I often
find it hard
to swallow
much of what
I'm fed.

I got hands
soft from
lack of labor
callused fingers
yes
but only by
the subtle grain
of poetry
music
and art.

I've got eyes
that know
the width of now
feeling every
color
if only
slightly less
in clarity.

I've a voice
that's loud
and clear
(mostly)
but often
reckless
and never
shy
and never one
to whisper
anything.

A MIGHTY CLAN

This is a
mighty clan
that gathers
here
before a
gray-matter
sea of
rhythm
and verse.

These bards
and skalds
do sing
with voices
pure and
real
of various
shades
and hues.

These prophets
of a new
religion
a philosophy
a state of
MIND.

How they fill
the ether
with their
pain
joy
hopes
dreams
and breath.

Their testaments
written here
in blood
generate gravity
of soul.

Attraction
of such heavenly
bodies
psalms to us
This covenant
of voice.

NO ONE KNOWS HER NAME

Cause around here
no one knows
her name.

She says,
"I'm so tired
of being tired"
to no one
unparticular
cause there's
no one there
to listen
anyway.

She keeps
thumbing through
that old brown
photo album
looking for
a reason
for her
to try and
carry on.

And all the while
the rain outside
keeps talking
to the wind
a private joke
they share
surely at her
expense.

And the night
that fits her
so uncommonly
well
will carry her
breath
away

with one last
heart beat
for the pipers
time
a dirge
of silent
prayer.

Cause around here
no one knows
her name.

COMMON JOYS

I have
in my life
murdered
common joys
in the pursuit
of selfish
desires

OWL-EYED MALAISE

There was a time
    when I
just wouldn't rhyme
    when I would
get out and prowl
through the night
like an owl
thought it might
help me howl
    like Ginsberg
but that was absurd
you see in a word
it just didn't
    "go"
just goes to show
you gotta go
    with the flow
even though
I just ain't no
Boxcar Jumper
any leg humper
proud chest thumper
    roustabout
    lout
throwing my clout
all about
I gotta get out
    of these shoes
try on another
some kind of blues

somebody who's
      rhythm has soul
some real rock 'n' roll
take a double fretted
Chuck Berry stroll
      on down to
Strawberry Fields
and lose myself
      out
      in the cellos.
And what strange fellows
working their bellows
and filling me full 'o
      hot air.
What do I care
I try not to stare
but it's hard when they're
      out there all day
making their pay
and like Tori say
      "I believe in peace"
      "Yeah, I believe in peace—Bitch"
and somewhere in the crease this
stories getting lame
cause it's the same
      old game
its just got another name
last time it was Vietnam
next time maybe old Tehran.

STATION BOOKSTORE

I remember
how I'd ride
that old
blue bike
driving
the peddles
in long
fluid strokes
down
and around
and on to the
old Station
Bookstore
where my best
friends mother
used to work.

Day after day
after school
and weekends too
my allowance
in hand
or the meager
earnings
from chucking
papers
I passed through
those heavy
darkly varnished
doors

and entered
my childhood
wonderland
come to life.

I remember
the sweeping
shape of it.
The deep
dark shelves
and cottage quaint
tables
all laid out
with knick-knacks
incense
candles
and cards

and books
books
books
books
novels and tombs
of every size
and weight.
Hard
and softbound
librams
of numerous
and untold
tales
a sea of writ
for me
to swim in.

I discovered
Middle Earth there
and followed
Hazel's tale.
Learned magic
on the Isle of Roke
and visited lands
beyond
the wardrobe.

For me
it was
that first real
place
that special
somewhere
that was mine
in my own
right
my first real
haunt.

In the end
its life was
shorter even
than my youth
and lives on now
only in my
dreams.

MENTORS

It was Tolkien
who first taught me
how to read.
It was Lennon
who first showed me
how to sing and dream.

I learned
the art of melody
from Emily
and my sense
of rhythm from Edgar
Allen Poe.

It was Paul
Simon that showed me
the world
but It was, Elizabeth
Browning that taught
me of love.

And it was both
Ginsberg and Rimbaud
who taught me of freedom
but I learned
the nature of art
From E.E.Cummings.

It was Dylan
who showed me
what life was about
and Monet
that showed me
how it all blends together.

I fathomed
the power of voice
from F. Scotts Fitzgerald
but I learned of
expression of soul
from Sylvia Plath.

THE DIVINE PALATE

The felling of trees
does not define me
present
or otherwise.

My voice
clamors
loudly before
the deaf eyes
of eternity
with the blood
red scent
of salt
and earth
I have touched
the divine palate
with blasphemous
thought.

ACCOMPLICES

We are a nation
of accomplices
apathetic viewers
of the evening news
sitting in idle
mass consumption
as crime after
horrific crime
plays out
in 30 second
sound-bites
or voicelessly scroll
across the bottom
while empty
talking heads
bury us in fear
and mountains
of meaningless
shit.

A STIRRING

Do I sense
...a stirring?

A dim
vibration
just there
below the
static?

Do I begin
to hear
a softness
of voices
a long slumbering
sound,
but beginning
to coalesce
forming
syllables
in the
empty corners
of night?

Oh you
villains
of industry

all you
fat-cat
lying
heads…

Beware!

For I have
heard
a thunder growing
softly yes,
but gaining
voice

and very soon
all your
hallowed halls
will echo
and shutter

for this
chorus of souls
has grown
weary of your
greedy lies.

It is the tempest
born of winds
of your own
devices
that very soon
It will cleanse
this dirty
scene.

ACHERON'S COURSE

I stand resolute at the edge of night
screaming countless stars and comets
out into the void and gaping maw of
eternities insufferable indifference.

I could paint with every shade of red
and still not fathom the nature of God
as he lends his ever pregnant pearl white
to the grim black landlords of Gehenna
        that bleed them out to Acheron's course.

No silver grasping boatman I
      no
I've not feet for aught but land.

SENSE OF FLOW

Are you ready?
        Let's go
                and flow
don't you know
        I got something
                to show
        you
I got something
        to blow
                you
        away

OK
whatever
        you say
                but today
I don't play
        like that.

                My old
        brown hat
just ain't
        where it's at
                and that
just doesn't
        make sense
                now, does it?

Oh well
        miss or hit

I was sure
        that I had it
before I started
        this bit
well don't get
        in a snit
I'm sure it
        will fit
if you jiggle it
                just a bit
oh shit
        it don't fit
                well that's it
        I just quit.

FLICKER

The candle
flicker…
flicker…
flickers
and kisses the night
with smoke.

Before I spoke
I thought I saw a rhythm
something oddly given
without hands
can you understand
it's nothing
that I planned
it just is…

or was
I should say?

Strange that this
is all I could pay
in the way of
a compliment
for something
so very
on top of it.

I feel incompetent
to express my
sentiment
on such a
sweet moment.

I'd own it
if I could
sure I would.

But I should
know better
Nothing lasts
forever
or at least
that I have ever
heard.

WALTZ

This tune
though it
struck only
A-minor chord
it plays in
A-major way
without a
diminished 6th
sense
it keeps
3
4
time
to the rhythm
of this
slow lilting
waltz.

GEM

I have swallowed
a sea of pearls
in search of
a single
precious gem
finely cut
and
ruby red
as the courses
of my ways.

Fairer souls
draped in splendors
grand and expansive
as horizons
faded
all rust
and tangerine.

There are
the silhouettes
of royal carrion
loitering
in the round
for whom
death holds
no mysteries
but life
hungers them
in the
wing.

And though
opals
I have known
cleverly smooth
and fair
to see

or alien
onyx
cruel in
its deviant
ways

still my gem
out reaches
me
my grasp
but childlike
and lame.

VEGAS

We were young in Vegas
proud, bold and ready
to claim our part
of the American dream
(such that it was)
We watched MTV
Vedder and Cobain
we loved the new music
that our older friends
found scary and strange
but we just laughed.

Laughing days
Vegas in summer
      HOT!
and dry mouth valley of sin
the endless parade of
peacock people and
the tortured singing of nickels
dimes and quarters
      cascading
into tin pan
or plastic cup
      cascading
and there was a strange rhythm
hard to find—like jazz
but all around
      mesmerizing.

We sank easily into motion
caught in each other's gravity
and we talked our night
straight into day
        -morning-
and the sun back up to torture
that broken land
stuck back together
with casinos and glue.

        When I left to go home
        I took you with me
        not right away physically
        but immediately in soul
        -gravity again-
        our orbits narrowed.

We went back to Vegas
        later to wed.
The little chapel
that now is gone
like so many of that city's
        landmarks
swallowed up by her ravenous need
for something new—something.
She is a fickle bitch
shallow and mean
but still fun at night
        all painted up.
Her little islands of foe culture;
fake New York to fake Parie'
we liked all the flowers
        at the Bellagio
        sweet censor

lunch at an indoor-outdoor cafe'
under a noon night sky
the air conditioned cool
keeping the desert heat
      at bay.

Printed in the United States
62801LVS00004B/4-12